It Always Seems Impo

Blank Notebook For To-Do Lists, Notes and Ideas

Prep work for Kitchen

- Paint Arm Rails
- Touch up cabinets
- Paint BASEBOARDS

Made in the USA
Middletown, DE
23 October 2018